Jamie And the Flower Contest

(A Story of High School Adventures)

BY

Grace Shobola

Legal Disclaimer

This is a work of fiction. Unless otherwise indicated, all the names, characters, businesses, places, events and incidents in this book are either the product of the author's imagination or used in a fictitious manner. Any resemblance to actual persons, living or dead, or actual events is purely coincidental.

This book or parts thereof may not be reproduced in any form, stored in any retrieval system, or transmitted in any form by any means—electronic, mechanical, photocopy, recording, or otherwise—without prior written permission of the Author.

If you would love to purchase additional copies of this book or reach the author, call or email.
+12812586749 | +234 807 531 0645
Email: graceshoproject@gmail.com

Published by
Marmax Publishing
www.maxwelloyewumi.ng/publish
+27739447483

TABLE OF CONTENT

Chapter One 01
The Sleepover

Chapter Two 6
Big Announcement

Chapter Three 12
Bad Cook, New Friends

Chapter Four 29
Harsh + Crazy = Mean Aunt

Chapter Five 49
Learning How to Swim

Chapter Six 64
Cheaters

Chapter Seven 71

Inspiration

Chapter Eight 78

Long Time No See

Chapter Nine 85

Bloom

Chapter Ten 92

Winners Got to Win, Losers Got to Lose

CHAPTER ONE

The Sleepover

"Jamie, wake up! Wake up! Aunty Midge is giving birth now!" Jamie's mom shook her a little roughly. Jamie was a deep sleeper.

"What?" Jamie said rubbing her eyes and looking around the room with a frown on her face. She sat up slowly.

"There is going to be a surgery. She has a problem with the umbilical cord. She needs support so –

Jamie came fully awake. "Can I come, mom? I am going with you?"

"No, no, Jamie! Totally out of the question. You are going to Anna's. The last time I took you the hospital you crawled to our room every time telling me that you had nightmares because of being in the hospital."

"That was when you were seven. You told me you hated hospitals."

"Mom, I am fourteen and not a baby anymore," Jamie protested.

"That's it! You are going to Anna's, and that's final."

"But, mom – "

"No buts. When I say final, I mean final."

Yes, mom. At least Anna's house isn't bad. Plus, she's my best friend. I do want to talk to her about school."

"Now that's my good girl. Let's go," Jamie's mother said to her.

* * *

At Anna's

"Anna, we need a new member," Jamie said. "We're six and need either seven or eight people. I am not in your school or in your club," Jamie went on totally ignoring Anna's response. "What does Sasi have that we don't?" she asked.

"Well, they have free chocolate. Besides, if I was in your school and didn't know anything about Sasi, I would have joined her club," said Anna.

"Ha Ha! Very funny, Anna! Come on! Being hygienic is better than having free chocolate," Jamie said.

"You're overreacting. I mean the school is getting a lifetime supplies of chocolate. You said so yourself. So, come off it," Anna said.

"Come off it, come off it. This club is very, very important to me," said Jamie.

"Okay, okay, okay! Don't get angry; you are very funny. When you are angry you turn red and your hair stands on end," said Anna.

"Okay, I guess you're right. Sometimes I overreact. I think I just can't pronounce it. I mean they can't just stop the club," said Jamie.

"Now let's get this sleepover started," Anna said. She knew Jamie could not stay up late. She loved to watch movies late into the night while Jamie seemed to have an internal clock; as soon as it chimed a particular hour, she must sleep. Tonight, however, in about two minutes, they had both drifted off to sleep.

The Next Morning

"Good morning, Jamie!" her mother greeted.

"Mom, how am I back home? Why am I here? I thought I was at Anna's place. I thought you went to meet Aunty Midge you and dad."

"Well, Aunty Midge gave birth early; and, while we came to pick you up, we found you asleep. So, I carried you," Jamie's dad said.

"Dad, I am in high school now. I am not a baby anymore," she complained with a playful frown.

"Well, you'd better hurry or you are going to be late for school," Jamie's mom told her.

"Oh no! I am sorry. Let me get ready," Jamie said as she entered the bathroom.

"Get your car ready, honey. She doesn't have a license to drive and you don't want her to be late to you know," Jamie's mom said to her husband.

CHAPTER TWO

Big Announcement

"Okay, everybody, I have a big announcement! Next month we're going to celebrate, on the first day of spring, the leader of the school. Members should meet me in my office," the principal said.

"Sorry, I am late. Somebody pushed me down," Sasi giggled. She and Jamie were best friends until Jamie realized that Sasi only cared about herself and the most expensive things.

"Okay, tell me what you want your decorations to be like. But please let them be full of flowers.

You may leave but Jamie, hold on, I need to talk to you in private," the principal said.

"Now, Jamie, you need more members," the principal observed when other students had left.

"I know, ma'am."

"Well, if you don't do that in two days, I will have to shut down your scout club. Anyway, I hope you do some big decorations. You may take your leave."

Immediately, Jamie opened the door. Sasi laughed at her. Guessing that Sasi had been spying on her, Jamie quickly ran out before Sasi could talk.

She knew she had to find somebody to talk into joining the scout club soon. Jamie ran to her class before she got late for that.

At Jamie's Club Meeting

"Hello, Leader Jamie!" everyone chorused.

"Okay, everyone, we have a big problem," Jamie said trying to catch her breath.

"What is it?" Dave asked.

"Well, if we can't find one more person to join our group in two days, we may have to disband our crew," Jamie said. All eyes were on her. Suddenly, she wished she hadn't told them anything. But it was the right thing to do, she told herself. There was a little silence. Then somebody broke it.

"Maybe we should go to Sasi and beg her to see if we can join her own club. It is better than nothing; right?" scout Finn said.

Nobody could blame him. He was one of those kids who followed Sasi everywhere. She was very attractive, plus her rich background made her famous. Even though she was spoilt and cruel, she still had followers everywhere. Also, Finn's statement did make sense. Joining Sasi's club was better than nothing.

Jamie could hear whispering around her. Everyone but she knew that everybody was thinking of joining Sasi's club. Again, it was better than nothing if all didn't turn out well. But she prayed it would end well. She cleared her throat to get everybody's attention.

"Does anybody have flowers?" she asked, trying to change the subject. There was a hush in the room before all hands shot up except Finn's. "Okay, I want each of you to bring flowers in five days to the school's greenhouse, that is, if we are permitted or our club is not closed down by then.

The bell rang.

"Okay, everybody! This meeting is over," Jamie announced.

Everybody ran out. Finally, school was over for the day. As Jamie walked towards the school's doors, Anna was smiling. Jamie smiled back.

"Hi Jamie! Why are you so gloomy?"

"Nothing," Jamie said.

"After the last time . . ." Anna began.

Then Jamie gave up and told Anna everything.

"Woah! But you are like the best there. The school cannot go cruising without you," Anna said.

"I know. But I don't make the rules. That's even what the principal said. The worst part is that some people are planning to go to Sasi's club," Jamie said.

"Okay, girl, I have good and bad news. The good one is that my school had to take the cafe and sports game area away to save money."

"How is that good news?" Jamie asked.

"Well, I am coming to your school."

"What!" Jamie shouted and jumped up and hugged Anna. "I don't even know how to thank you enough."

"Well, you are doing pretty well," Anna said trying to breathe.

"Sorry, what's the bad news?" Jamie asked, looking serious.

"It's already a day out of the two days you were given," Anna said.

"Sorry, girl, it's okay," Jamie said, smiling. "I can ask the principal for more time. She isn't hard but is very nice actually."

Jamie and Anna walked towards their houses and said goodbye to each other at their junction. Jamie entered the house and found a note on the dining table. It was from her mom, and it said:

"Jamie, if you are reading this, your dad and I are going to be really late. So, there's a pizza in the oven that you should eat. Also, throw away the trash."

Jamie sighed. She ate a slice of the pizza and then went outside. She felt the wind on her skin as it rushed past her. Soon she went inside and threw herself on the bed. Just before she dozed off, she thought to herself, "only if I could spend more time with my parents!"

CHAPTER THREE

Bad Cook, New Friends

"Good morning, mom," Jamie greeted.

"Good morning, Jamie. How was your night?" her mom responded.

"Fine, mom. How about yours?" Jamie asked.

"It was fine, thank you," Jamie's mom said with a smile. You are having cornbread for dinner and for school."

Jamie smiled. Her mother was nicknamed Mrs. Clean because of her high level of hygiene. She remembered that one day, while she was in kindergarten, she saw a fly in her food and the school's cook told her to remove it and eat the food. And, of course, she did. When she told her mom, her mom was very unhappy about it. Since then, she made sure Jamie had homemade food even when Jamie changed schools.

Her dad came in.

"Good morning, my daughter," he said as he hugged Jamie. And my beautiful wife," he said as he left Jamie and went to his wife and kissed her.

"Good morning, dad," Jamie greeted.

"It is time to go to school and I don't want her to be late," Jamie's mom said to her husband.

"Bye, mom. Love you," Jamie said, rushing to her dad's car parked outside. "Come on, dad, I don't want to be late," she said.

"Well, I'd better take the kid to school," Jamie's dad said to his wife.

Inside the car, everywhere was quiet such that they could hear the tires grinding against the tarred road as the car sped along.

"Sorry about yesterday," Jamie's dad said to her. Jamie wished her dad didn't have to talk so honestly all the time. She just hated questions sometimes. She was quiet for a little time. Then she said in a low voice:

"Oh, it was nothing."

"I know you are sad about it but I promise that your mother and I will try to make time for you," her dad said.

"Thanks, dad."

"And sorry about not having any new members in your club," Jamie's dad said.

"How did you – " Jamie began. "Did mother –"

"Yeah, she did," said Jamie's dad.

Jamie pulled out a small recording device from her math book. "Dang it! Why did she have to take her math book with her to the principal's office?" she thought to herself.

"Well, dad, you keep it," Jamie said. Then they were at the school. Jamie left the device in the car for her dad. She looked at him; he was trying to act casual since it was going to record anything he said. "Bye, dad," Jamie said as she got out of the car and walked towards the school gate. *Up Pine College*, said a big sign.

Her school opened in 1865. It wasn't the best but its teaching was very good although it didn't have money to pay teachers regularly and ended up owing so many people. But the charity service helped. Some orphanage children attended the school without paying fees. But the principal would not allow that to continue. So, he sold the school to a rich merchant. Now, the rich merchant did not want to pay the debts but also did not want the school to fall apart. So, he accepted to pay the debts. It did not stop there; he also made the teaching level higher. Then one day, he sold it to a woman.

Jamie was thinking about all of these things when she felt someone pull her ponytails.

"Hello pony!" Jamie heard a voice say. She turned around and saw Sasi.

"Haha! Very funny, Sasi," Jamie said, trying to smoothen her hair with her hand.

"You know, Jamie, one thing I don't like about pigs is they are always so dirty," Sasi said as she entered the school.

Jamie then followed. "Hi Mrs. Freckles," she said as she entered the staff room, "dad said he will bring the flowers in the afternoon.

"Okay," Mrs. Freckles said. Her dad had promised her a bunch of cotton flowers. She was also Jamie's tailor.

Jamie went up to her class for History. As she walked, Mrs. Freckles smiled at her. "What a respectful girl!" she thought.

Jamie And the Flower Contest

Jamie sat at her desk. It was test time on History. The teacher wrote out the question on the chalkboard.

This time, they scattered the tables because, in the last test, Sasi had copied Lisa's work and they both had to go to detention (actually Lisa went because Sasi's dad complained about it but mostly Sasi's dad was under her control). Soon the test was over. All the scripts were marked and returned to their owners. Then Jamie got a little peek at Sasi's book and saw that she scored 1/20. "OMG! Is she good at anything at all?" Jamie wondered.

Then the bell rang. It was lunchtime.

The crowd in the lunch room was much. Jamie sat alone like always. She didn't have any friends in school. So, she mostly sat alone by the window. Then she saw Sasi coming to her table. "Maybe she is coming to sit with somebody close to her," Jamie thought and concentrated on her food. But then Sasi sat on her table without permission and said:

"Okay, Jamie, I will give you this option now. So, if you close down now and join my club not only will I welcome you but you will be the new Vice President; and you know they both get free jobs and a full bag of cookies. You know it will be better than nothing. Right, Jamie?"

"Sasi, don't you remember we broke up for a reason and we will be fighting all the time if we are in the same club? So, no," Jamie said.

"And just to inform you, Finn said he is going to join my club as soon as your club shuts down. It's just one more day. Think about it," Sasi said as she wiped her mouth with Jamie's napkin that she snatched from her table. She then went back to her seat to join her pack of girls.

Jamie sighed. At least she wouldn't be thinking about walking to her house. Her parents will pick her up in the evening.

Jamie And the Flower Contest

After school, Jamie waited for her parents to pick her up. After a short while, the secretary called her.

"Your mother is here."

"Thank you, ma'am," Jamie told her. She went downstairs with her, then saw her mom looking pale.

"Hi mom!" Jamie greeted. But her mom only nodded.

"Mom, is something wrong?" she asked.

"No, dear, nothing's wrong," Jamie's mom said. It seemed it was even hard for her to talk. They ended up not talking at all in the car on the ride home. When they got to their neighborhood, Jamie smelled something burning. She got scared. There was no fire unless . . .

"Mom, is dad cooking?" Jamie asked suddenly.

Her mom sighed. "Yes, he is," she answered.

"Why would you let him do that?!" Jamie asked.

"I didn't, but he refused to hear anything I said," her mom replied.

* * *

"Dad, we're home," Jamie said as she entered the house.

"Well, sit down, honey, 'cause I made dinner. It is ready and you are just in time," her dad said with pride in his voice.

"Mom's here," Jamie said as she opened the door for her dad to see her mom; but he couldn't see through all that smoke.

"Go and sit down and rest," he told her gently. "Dinner will be served in five minutes."

"Okay, dad," Jamie said. She and her mother sat down at the dinner table.

"What should we do to the food? We can't hide it in our shoes, can we?" Jamie asked her mom in a whisper.

"Maybe. But keep calm; we might taste some," said her mom.

"Here is the dinner," Jamie's dad said as he walked towards them with a tray of food. It was smoked fish and sauce with macaroni and cheese.

"Mmmm! Dad, this looks delicious. I guess it will taste great," Jamie said.

Her mom forced a smile while looking at the food. Then she took a piece of the food and directed it to her mouth.

"It's good," she said.

"Sorry, I need to wash my hands," Jamie's dad said.

As soon as he went to the kitchen, Jamie's mom said to her daughter: "I have some plastic cups here," and handed her one.

"The food is burnt and disgusting," Jamie said as she dumped two spoonfuls in the cup. When the small cup was full, she asked her mom: "Where are we putting this?"

"Under the table," her mom replied.

Let me . . . oh my! You have almost finished your food," her dad said with excitement as he returned from the kitchen.

"Yes, we have," said Jamie, putting a piece of the smoked fish in her mouth. "Very delicious," she managed to say. She wanted to vomit but needed to finish everything at once. "I need water," she said and left the dining table while taking her plate with her.

"Oh God! That tastes like rotten shoe!" she exclaimed as soon as she was alone. It reminded her of the time Sasi tricked her into eating a soggy shoe and said it was a piece of chicken. It did smell like chicken. And then Jamie found out the truth. She also said she was sorry she was mean and it was a token to say sorry. That was one horrible chicken and a mean token. Anna had a stack of dreams on a shelf which came through (yep that was a total lie; she wished she could throw a thing at Sasi's face). She hoped it was real. Maybe she needed a shelf too. Well, her dream will be a big tank of water to pour on her to make her all wet and soggy for the soggy boot.

"Jamie! Are you okay?" her mom asked her.

"Yeah, I am fine, thank you. I am going to my room," Jamie said.

"Wait," her mom said. "It's family game night."

"Yes, it is," Jamie and her dad said at the same time. Her mom gave her dad a look. Her dad squeezed his face.

"Jamie, you choose. What do you want?" her mother asked.

"One thing I never want to change is that when you do something to make someone sad, you have to make it up to them," Jamie said as she rubbed her hands mischievously. "I choose chess, and I'm playing with dad."

"I am Jamie's supporter," her mom said quickly. "And I will get the drinks. Anyway, do you want smart chess juice, hon?"

"Good one, mom," Jamie said.

"It is not funny," her dad said.

"Oh yes, it is," Jamie said.

"Oh no, it is not," her dad said.

"Oh yes, it is," Jamie insisted.

Her dad sighed. "This is not going to end well," he murmured to himself. He was not very good at chess.

"This is so going to end well," Jamie said out loud. She had heard him.

"How did you do that?" her dad asked when she made a move on the chessboard.

"Come on, dad. I won. Plus, it was a knight. It's meant to be moved in an L-shape pattern. Let's play again."

"This is the tenth time. It's time for me to sleep but – "

Before her dad could finish his sentence, she dashed to the stairs. She could hear her mom.

"I told you she would win," she said.

"You were supporting your daughter instead of your husband," her dad said.

"Well, clean the table," her mother said to her.

Then Jamie went to sleep totally forgetting that her club may be closed down the next day. She would only remember in the morning.

At School

Jamie felt all sweaty and uncomfortable. She said to herself that everything was going to be alright.

"Hello everybody! Today we have a new student, two actually," Mr. Murphy said.

"Well, it's about time a student new came," Jamie thought.

"You all should sit down while I call out their names," Mr. Murphy said. "This is Jamie," he said pointing to the new girl.

"We have another Jamie here," said Sasi, pointing to her Jamie.

"Well, you can call me Jane," the new girl said.

"Then this is Preston," Mr. Murphy said, turning to the boy.

"Well, go to your seats," said Mr. Murphy.

Jamie didn't know why but Sasi seemed so distracted and she was distracted looking at Sasi looking at the new boy. She even called him to sit close to her.

"Woah," thought Jamie. She did not want to say his name.

"Alright, the people who got 20 and 19 in the math test, come out," said Mr. Murphy.

Jamie stepped out. She was disappointed she got 19. It was a trick question that stopped her from scoring 100%. She was jealous, really mad, and she turned red-hot that the boy (whose name she found hard to pronounce) could get the answers to all 20 questions correctly.

At The Principal's Office

"Jamie, I know I said two days," said the principal. "But since we have two new students and our rule says they should join at least one club so they can warm up to the school, you have to ask them tomorrow."

Jamie was happy Sasi was there to hear that. Sasi looked like she was going to tear the principal into pieces but still smiled. Jamie wondered how on earth she was going to stop herself from tearing her apart because she did not like her forced smile. Now what could she do to change her mood? she asked herself.

"Okay, I know spring is not far; it is just next month," said Mr. Murphy. "So, I want you girls to compete against each other. So, I want a stage –"

"Sorry, sir, what kind of competition?" Jamie asked.

"Why didn't you say that before 'sorry but what kind of competition'?" Sasi said, intending to put Jamie in a spot.

"Sorry. I didn't say so," Jamie said.

"Girls, I think it will be more exciting to have a kind of contest that is not usual: a flower contest. So, please plant beautiful flowers and I will be glad for whoever wins."

"I already know who is going to win," Sasi said as soon as they got out of the office. "It's me."

"Well, you don't know that. I am sure you don't even know what to plant; and, because your dad is so rich, he will pay for a topnotch gardener to do it for you."

"And you, big mouth," Sasi said as she turned and rubbed her hand in Jamie's face, then went away to class.

Jamie had to go to class so that she would not be late. She had thought it couldn't get worse between her and Sasi but it did.

In English class, it happened again. So, in History, General Knowledge, Science, Geometry and all other subjects, why was she always second and Preston first? she wondered. She wanted to scream at him and tear him apart because today just wasn't her lucky day.

CHAPTER FOUR

Harsh + Crazy = Mean Aunt

Closing Time

"Jamie, how are you doing? Did you have a bad day?" Anna asked.

"How did you know?" Jamie replied in surprise.

"Well, your face is grayish pink and you are fair; it makes you look odd," Anna said, "like the day you –"

Jamie covered her mouth before she could say more. "Okay," she began as she removed her hand from Anna's mouth, "we have two new kids in class, a boy and a girl. Now, I don't want attention but the boy keeps coming first in all our tests I am always coming second."

"Ha!" exclaimed Anna.

"What's funny?" Jamie asked.

"You don't get, Jamie. That part that you said you don't want attention, it's obvious you want more attention. Plus, what is bad about coming second like I who comes second, third or fourth? So, it's a total joke; mostly, it's a lie."

"Well, Anna, you are saying it is not a big problem. I might not get into a good college or university if my scores are not good."

"Okay, Miss Good College," Anna said. "Anyway, how near is your aunt's house? It looks like a million miles."

"After the corner," Jamie said.

"It's hot out here," Anna complained. Just then a car stopped in front of them. "Jamie, look! It stopped for us," Anna said while dragging Jamie to the car and ignoring her protest.

"Anna, you know how much I hate going into people's cars," Jamie said, continuing to protest. They both got to the car when Jamie saw Preston at the steering wheel. Jane was in the passenger seat.

"Hey! Want a ride?" Preston asked them.

"Cool. Is that the boy you were talking about? Woah! He even has a car," Anna said. "Since he's in your school, he's not a stranger. Cool car," Anna said to Preston.

Jamie knew Anna was right: Preston was not utterly a stranger. Then she snapped out of what she was thinking before she was tempted to enter the car. "Thanks," she said.

"Jamie, are you coming too?" Anna asked. She was already inside.

Jamie wanted to turn and walk away. "Anna, of all people, knows I wouldn't get into the car even if it is the only way to save my life," Jamie thought. "Or maybe I would enter the car if it was a matter of life and death." "Okay, fine," Jamie said aloud, changing her mind. She couldn't bear seeing Anna and Jane's hopeful eyes any longer. Jane looked like she wanted Jamie to come in and if she didn't, she could faint and Anna . . . Well, she couldn't say no to her. She entered the car.

"Where are you going?" Jane asked her as soon as she got in.

"Well, around the corner," Anna said. "And Jamie will tell you where to go." It was Jamie's turn to glare at Anna.

Anna glared back and whispered "What?"

"Never mind," Jamie said sighing, trying to smile to show everything was alright.

"Sorry, I know you don't like talking much," Anna said.

"It's okay," Jamie told her. "Here is where you are going to: turn left and go down the road close to a bakery, then go right. If you see a flag, you have gone too far. Then just go through the roundabout, take a left turn and stop at the third block."

"Woah! How can you remember all of that?" Jane asked.

"She memorized it through a song," Anna said.

"Oh! Big bro does that too," Jane said.

"Big bro, big bro. Oh you mean him?" Anna said, nodding towards Preston. "I am confused. Your brother?" Anna said.

"Well, we are not twins. But I was born a year and 5 minutes after him. So, he's older and I call him big bro. Right, brooo?" Jane asked Preston, giggling. It was clear to Jamie that Preston hated the word and Jane was using it to tease him.

"Jane, for the millionth time, stop calling me that," Preston said. "Call me by my name. It is not hard to pronounce."

"Okay, I will not say that word again," Jane promised.

"Thank y –" Preston started to say.

"Only when I don't see you, man," Jane said with a straight face.

"You hit him!" Anna said, high-fiving Jane.

"It is going to be a long day," Preston muttered to himself. That was the same thing Jamie thought. She would rather tell her father to cook for her than to be in this car. She just had to sacrifice her taste buds; it might even make her sick. At least, that would be an excuse for not entering the car.

Then the car pulled over. "Here we are," Preston said, pointing to a flat.

"Yes, this is the house, thank you," Jamie said, opening the door before Preston could get out and do it for her. "Anna, I I sure had enough of that."

Anna nodded, not to show she was on Jamie's side but to tell her it was fun. Now she turned to Preston and Jane. "Hey, you guys want to drink cold tea in Jamie's aunt's house?"

"No, we're okay," Preston replied.

"Thank goodness!" Jamie thought. She couldn't imagine what her aunt would say if they had said yes. She would probably call her mom who will then inform the school that, "hello, my child is never coming to your school again. She was trying to get attention saying 'hello, I am right here. Can I get attention?'" And then she was waving her hands, saying, "mom, I don't want to leave Pine High School. The club . . . it's my career." Then her mom will say, "Stop this. Honey; you are misbehaving." Then her life will be torn to shreds.

"Jamie! Jamie! Are you okay?" she heard someone ask her from a long way off. "I will go get some water," she heard another voice say. "Jamie, wake up please," she heard Anna say. "Please wake up. Please!

"What?" Jamie asked in confusion as she regained consciousness.

"I got the water," someone said.

No, wait!" Anna said. But it was too late. Her aunt slipped and a bowl of water was poured on Jamie. First, Jamie was shivering in the cold; then she fainted again while trying to put herself together.

Happily, she regained consciousness a few minutes later.

"Jamie! Oh my God! Girl, never you faint on me again. You gave me a scare. You promised!"

"Anna, dear, let's give Jae a rest. Anyway, I have hot cocoa," Jane said.

"Woah! You have a cool Aunt Jae," Anna whispered.

"Jae, Jae, Jae. What kind of name is that?" Jane wondered.

"Ohhh! That was Jamie's nickname when she was little. Well, boy, that was a bad nickname.

Anna came up. "Want some hot coco? It's delicious. You've got to try it, girl," she said.

Jamie nodded. She didn't feel like talking even though she wanted to know some things. Anna knew what happened to her: how she fainted and why. But, hot cocoa . . . it was delicious.

"Yeah, I am not really hungry," Jamie said. Her stomach couldn't take anything hot or she could vomit. And, Anna, if she ever listened to the online videos that their parents made them watch (which Anna found boring; so, she slept off while watching them, snoring, after saying "this is boring" a hundred times, and Jamie had to cover up for her because Anna's parents really wanted Anna to watch it).

"Yea, free chocolate. Sorry, Jamie, if you are feeling sick. But, hey, free chocolate mmm," Anna said. "Look, Jamie! Isn't it beautiful? It has a picture of a girl like you."

"See your ponytail. My own was a star mmm," Jamie said, teasingly.

Anna wanted to put her hand on the creamy picture and lick it.

"Yeah. Don't put your hand on it," Jamie said. "You gave it to me."

Anna stuck her tongue out at Jamie, and so did Jamie. "Let's go to the parlor," Anna said.

"It's called a living room," Jamie said.

Ohhh Jamie! Stop being such a grandma borer," Anna said.

"Borer?" asked Anna. "Not a word in this case. Mr. Tickle Crab said so."

"Who?" Jamie asked.

"Get her," Anna said as she tickled Jamie to the floor.

"Stop, stop it. Anna, stop it," Jamie said.

"Not if you go to the parlor; and no correction of that word," Anna said.

"Oh, Anna," Jamie said. As she got to the sitting room, she saw her aunt staring at the pages of a magazine.

"Perfect couple," the lady said. Then she stared at a woman on another page like "I will get you even if it is the last thing I do!" Then Jamie recognized a man holding the woman who looked familiar to her.

"What's up?" Anna whispered.

"That picture," Jamie replied, pointing.

"What about it?" Anna asked.

"It looks so familiar," said Jamie.

"You mean that guy from the CPC," said Anna.

"What is the CPC?" Jamie asked.

"The City Planning Commission," Anna answered.

"Yes. Now, I remember," Jamie said a little too loudly.

"Oh Anna Jae! I mean Jamie," Midge said, startled. "How long have you been there and what do you remember?"

"Oh! She remembers that she was going to cook for all of us tomorrow. Right?" Jamie said, giving

Anna an angry face. "That was all you had in mind. Oh! At least you said tomorrow."

Anna just shrugged.

"Oh, Jamie dear, how nice of you! You take after your mother. It must be a joy for her to have a brilliant and beautiful daughter like you – unlike my stupid baby," Midge said so loudly that the baby cried. Midge hissed. "Don't mind her; she's been crying all day. I have had enough of her."

"What if she's hungry?"

"Let her starve. Does she think it's easy to give birth, pay the hospital bills and give her food? I am sure she can't even work. Let me tell you: if I was pregnant for Jonny, Jonny's child would be much more well behaved. I should have gotten rid of that Celia girl when he was hanging out a lot with her. I will go check on her."

"Me too," Anna said.

Jamie whispered to Anna: "Don't ask. I will tell you later. When Jamie got to the baby's room, she looked around. Anna was the first to speak.

"Is this a room or a store? All I can see are boxes," Anna said. Then Jamie saw a baby in a big shirt and a hat.

"Is it – it's a girl. Her eyes are still closed a little," Jamie said as she carried the baby up. "You are a cutie, a little cutie," she said. The baby sneezed. "I guess you are hungry." She heard the baby's stomach rumble.

"Don't feed it!" Jamie's aunt called out. "Don't take any milk from my kitchen just to feed that thing."

"I have milk," Anna said.

"Okay, but put it in my bottle. It has water. Just shake it," Jamie said. "Here you go," she said to the baby.

"You haven't been getting much attention, have you," Anna said to the baby as she rubbed her cheeks. "Hey Jamie! Was it me or was your aunty going crazy?"

"Okay, sit on a box and let me tell you a story," Jamie told her. "My aunt dated Jonny from the CPC. He was very famous."

"Yay! He's hot," Anna said.

"So, Aunty Midge fell in love with him. But, one day, I spied on my mom. She thought they were planning on getting married. Then the sad news. Mom called to say thanks for taking care of her and that she knew she would be in good hands when they got married. But Jonny told her he was interested in her but not in love with her. He said that he was just a friend and she should not tell her sister because he had a fiancé already and wanted to get married to her. What he didn't know was that Aunty Midge was already planning on getting married herself. When she found out, he left her."

"But how about the baby?" Anna asked.

"As I was saying," Jamie said as she returned to the story. "Then she met my uncle and got pregnant for him. But she found out Jonny was in town. So, she ran after him and left my uncle. He's dead now."

"So, is that how she got the baby?" Anna asked.

"Yes," Jamie said. "Oh, that was Cassie he married."

"What's her name?" asked Anna.

"I don't know. Midge didn't even bother to have a naming ceremony anyway."

Anna said: "Let's clear these boxes."

Jamie opened a big box. It was full of baby stuff: two dresses, a pacifier and a cot. "You are sleeping in my room today," Jamie said. The baby sneezed. "Anna."

"Here," Anna said, giving Jamie a pillow to put inside the cot. "When I saw the cot was empty, I ran to your room to get a pillow. Was I fast? I am training for a race in town next week."

"Well, you are surely going to going to win, Anna," Jamie said. "That's what my mom says whenever I am running up and down in the house. She says I should practice in the open space because I might break something while I am running."

Anna had never been this excited when she won other races. But when Jamie said that she could come to her house to have tea, she started talking about how she had a friend but never invited her to anything, not even her birthday party. When she asked her why not, she just said she couldn't invite her to all parties and left. Jamie snapped out of her thoughts. Anna had stopped talking and was now carrying the cot.

"Let's take this to your room," Anna said. "And thanks for being the best friend ever."

"You too," Jamie replied.

"Let's get this to your room before your aunt finds out. Okay?" Anna said.

Anna carried the cot while Jamie carried some clothing so that she could change the baby's clothes. Thereafter, Jamie and Anna went downstairs to relax after Jamie had tucked in the baby who was now dressed in a new dress and was sleeping. Jamie and Anna sank into separate chairs. Taking care of a baby is hard, especially when you are trying to get them to bathe and wear new clothes, Jamie thought. They keep on crying and keep trying to get out by crying. Thank God her doors are soundproof: you can't hear what is going on inside from outside. If you want to call somebody, you'd have to use the intercom in front of the door.

Then the doorbell rang.

"I'll get it Jamie," said tiredly. She opened the door. "Congratulations, Mrs. – " She stopped in mid-sentence. Before her stood a teenage boy.

"H! Is Aunty Midge here?" the young boy asked and entered the house.

"Is that Scott I hear?" Aunty Midge asked, walking to the door. Jamie left the doorway for her aunt. She hugged Scott. "Come sit," he told him. "How is grandma?"

"She is fine," Scott answered.

"She treats him like her son but treats her own baby like a rag," Anna whispered to Jamie. Jamie hoped her aunt did not hear it because it was a harsh thing to say even though it was very true.

"Well, Scott, I'd like you to meet my niece, she the smart one I was telling you about," Aunty Midge said, introducing Jamie.

"Hi! Nice to meet you," Jamie said, smiling sweetly even though what she really wanted to say was goodbye.

"And this is her friend, Anna."

"Hey!" Anna said, not even a bit interested in the introduction.

"She is staying with us tonight. Right, dear?" Jamie said.

"Yes," Anna said.

"Well, you are welcome to stay here for as long as you like," Aunty Midge said to Anna as sweetly as she could. She is now pretending to be sweet, Jamie thought. But how can she be when she doesn't even care about her daughter?

"Well, I won't waste your time. Mrs. Sophie and Grandma Fae Fae said I should give this to you; it's for the baby," Scott said, handing over a basket to Aunty Midge. It was full of stuffed animal toys and Grandma Fae Fae's special soup. "I need to get to back to bed to get ready for school tomorrow," he added and said bye to them.

When he got to the door, he glanced back at them and then just vanished. At least, that was what Jamie thought. She was so tired. Her aunty and Scott had been talking for more than one hour, and it way past her bedtime which is 7:00 p.m. It was 8:00 p.m. when she told her aunt about it.

"Don't be rude, Jamie," her aunt said. "Sit down. At least, he is gone."

Jamie only murmured. Then her aunt said, "Bye."

"We're going to bed too," Anna told her friend. "We go to the same school."

Jamie had totally forgotten that Anna was coming to her school the next day. "Good night, Anna," she told her. "You don't have a sleeping bag."

"I do," Anna replied. "It's in my bag."

"In your bag?" Jamie asked in surprise.

"You can't go out without being prepared – even when going to school," Anna said. She learnt that from her scout club.

"Good night, Anna," Jamie said.

But Anna was already sound asleep in her sleeping bag.

"Good night to me," Jamie said to herself and slept.

CHAPTER FIVE

Learning How To Swim

Jamie woke up by 4 a.m. because the baby was crying. But Anna didn't hear anything; her iPods' earpiece was still in her ears. Jamie tried to wake Anna up but she just pushed her hand away. Then Jamie removed the earpiece from her friend's ears.

"I'm up! I'm up! What happened? Is there a thief in the house?" Anna asked. Jamie pointed to the baby.

"Okay, baby girl, what do you want?" Anna asked.

"I think it is time to feed the baby or change her diapers," Jamie said.

"Well, I ain't changing it," Anna replied. "You woke me up for this?"

"No, I woke you up to get milk to feed the baby while I change the diaper. There's still some in the bottle and it's enough to feed her," Jamie said.

"Where's the bottle?" Anna asked.

"Over there!" Jamie pointed.

"Thanks," Anna said.

"I will get the diaper. It is a good thing I packed it even though you said you won't need it," Jamie said.

"Don't rub it in," Anna said.

"Ha! Jealous," Jamie teased.

"Stop it!" Anna warned.

"Ha!" Jamie said.

"Oh my God!" Anna said. "Jamie, what happened to her eyes?"

"What do you mean?" Jamie asked, going over to Anna. "Adorable!"

"Look at her eyes! They are brown," Anna said. "It will only take three days."

Jamie looked at the baby again and was drooling. "Adorable," she repeated.

"No offense, Jamie. It's amazing how your aunt is a little well . . ."

Jamie covered Anna's mouth. "As much as you don't get it, I don't get it," she said. The baby burped. "We better get ready for school," she said.

Anna looked at the time. "It's just four o'clock," she said. "Who wakes up this early? I am going back to bed."

She entered her sleeping bag while Jamie prepared for school.

A Short While Later

"You woke up early," Midge told Jamie.

"Yeah. It's going to be a long walk to school," Jamie said.

"Oh! You can take my car. It's at the side," Midge said as she removed her car key from her keyholder.

"I can't drive," Jamie said.

"Nonsense. I saw you driving in the evening with your dad every time I came to your house. Don't worry, I won't tell your mom," Midge said.

"Okay, I will drive," Jamie said as she collected the car key and put it in her pocket. She didn't like some dangerous or extreme sports. But her father said driving was easy. So, he'd been teaching her how to drive a car.

Anna came down. "What are we having for breakfast?" she asked.

Jamie just looked at her as she grabbed an apple from the fruit bowl and tossed it in a bowl of water in the sink. "Oh! And good morning," Anna said as she bit into the apple.

"Energetic. I like you," Midge said and laughed.

Anna smiled. "I hear that from a lot of people. I am not sure why," Anna said as she threw the remainder of her apple into the air and kicked it into the dustbin. Jamie was not surprised anymore. She once saw Anna take a banana peel and flick it into the dustbin.

"I once joined an athletics competition," Anna said. "The judges did give me 10-10-9, and I won a trophy. But I was expecting a 10-10-10. I guess I tried. But I want to be perfect for the race."

"Keep eating before breakfast and you will be too full to eat anything," Midge told her.

"Don't worry," Anna said as she watched the bacon fry in the pan. "As long as it is as good as Jamie's mom's cooking, there will always be room in my stomach," she said, patting her stomach. But she didn't take another fruit.

"Cooking runs in the family. My sister was the best," Midge said. "Girl, if you are hungry, feast your eyes on this," she added as she served bacon and pancakes and poured maple syrup all over them. "It's good to let the syrup spread," she said.

Midge rested on the couch in the sitting room. Anna had gone out to pack her things. Jamie told her aunt.

"Oh! That's nice," Midge said. "I hope Emma didn't disturb you."

So, that's her name, Jamie thought to herself. "How did you know?" she asked.

"Well, every day she cries, and it tires me," Midge said. "When I didn't hear her, I guess you have taken her."

"Who is going to take care of her while we're busy with school?" Jamie asked her.

"Oh! I hired a babysitter yesterday. She should be good. She will cost me a million bucks," Midge said as she turned on the TV and kept pressing the TV remote as she checked different channels. Jamie watched her aunt for a few seconds before going to her room.

"Give it back," Jamie heard Anna say. She was dragging a hair band with Emma. Jamie laughed. Even though Anna was shouting at the baby, she was trying not to hurt her. "Give me, you baby," Anna said as she tried to collect her hair band from Emma. Jamie laughed and laughed.

After The Babysitter Came

"I can't believe we have to walk from here to school. It's 5 miles away I guess," Anna said, moaning.

"Not really. And we're in the front of her house," said Jamie as she took the key and swung it around her forefinger. "And I am driving."

"You can't drive," Anna said. "Aren't you afraid of dangerous sports anymore?"

"I have to. I promised Aunty Midge," Jamie said.

Anna smiled. "I always knew you have it in you," she said. "Where's the car?"

"There are a lot of cars here. That one," Jamie said pointing to a black car with silver rims.

"Cool! This has to be new. I am sure it costs a million dollars," Anna said. "My aunt used to be a rock star. She quit and became a nurse and then retired; and my uncle used to be very rich and he willed everything to her. I still don't get why but I have never said it and it's not a secret. Almost everybody in my street knows and a few know here," Jamie said as she opened the car door.

Anna sat in the front passenger seat. A couple of dark blue shades were in the front. Jamie and Anna looked at each other. One thing they both loved was wearing blue shades, the real ones.

* * *

Jamie parked the car in the school's parking lot and Anna got out.

"How come the school has a driveway for children?" Anna asked.

"Sasi has a car and this used to be the teachers' parking lot," Jamie said. "So, she forced them to give her the driveway. Or was it her dad? She controls him like a video game and she's the controller." Jamie removed her glasses. "They don't allow this in school," she said and put it back in the car.

"So, what kind of thing do you do today that's a sport?" Anna asked.

"Swimming," Jamie said. Then she watched Anna get out of the car and put the glasses back where they were meant to be. "I am sure your parents informed the principal about you. Just go straight to her office."

"Sure," Anna said as she carried her bag.

"Are you okay?" Jamie asked.

"I am fine," Anna said. "It's just that I really liked my old school. I am not so sure about this. It looks like they would never ride a cycle without safety gear and a wet slippery floor."

"They do that in your old school?" Jamie shouted.

"My parents don't know about it but yes. That's why a lot of people get broken bones," Anna said laughing. "And it's fun."

"You are not serious at all," Jamie said as she opened the school gate and went in.

* * *

Jamie and Sasi were called into the principal's office.

"So, girls, the principal began, "have you planted any plant? The party is in a few weeks."

"Oh no! I forgot," Jamie said. "I am so sorry."

"Don't worry," the principal told her.

Sasi was twisting her hair. "I also haven't started yet," she said." I am too busy. Yesterday I had to do my hair and my nails and I can't plant if my nails are wet."

Since Sasi's dad was the mayor of the city, the principal couldn't discipline Sasi or speak to her anyhow she pleased unless she wanted to get fired from her job, and with no retirement money.

"Excuse me," the principal said. She took the microphone. "Everyone, go to the bus that will take you to where you're meant to swim. Do that calmly as running or pushing is forbidden in the school hall. Thank you." She turned off the microphone. "Girl, show a little more effort in this," she said to Sasi. "You may go. And, Jamie, I like your friend's energy; but make sure she doesn't try to make a racing competition in school."

Jamie smiled. "Okay," madam.

Sasi looked at Jamie, hoping for an explanation.

"Sorry," Jamie said and walked away.

***

"So, where's the changing room?" Anna asked.

"There," Jamie pointed to a small place like a house.

"Aren't you coming?" Anna asked.

"In a minute," Jamie said. She looked at the pool. Who liked swimming if you could drown in it? she asked herself. She shivered and then caught up with Anna.

"I can't swim in this swimsuit. They said these are for new people. She said it," Anna said and pointed to Jane.

"Hi Jane," Jamie said. "Are you having trouble deciding?"

"No," Jane said. "I hate swimming. I mean, why on earth do you want to swim if you can . . ."

"Drown," Jamie said, completing the sentence for her. They both laughed.

"I choose that flaming-red one," Anna said.

"But how?" Sasi asked.

"The red motorcycle is a killer," Anna said. "Plus, I always wanted one since I had dreams of creaming sports."

Jamie and Jane laughed again.

"What's so funny?" Sasi asked.

When Jamie and Sasi were friends, she was always the one to make friends with ease. Girls came to her and said they wanted to be her friends.

"Jamie, I see you have made friends with the two new kids," Sasi said.

"Oh no!" Jamie said. "These are Anna and Jane," she said to annoy Sasi as if she didn't know their names. "Anna and I have known each other since. I thought you knew them."

"She became my friend just yesterday," Jane said. "My brother gave Anna a ride home. I don't know why you didn't enter the car."

"Jamie, Jane says she knows Anna longer than I have," said Sasi.

Sasi was red-hot with anger. "I need to change into my swimsuit," she said as she stomped away.

"Why did you say I didn't enter your car?" Jamie asked.

"Well, you didn't want to enter at first," Jane said. "So, if I told Sasi the truth, I am sure she will tell everyone; and I think that swimsuit with a rainbow is nice."

"That's nice. Thanks," Jamie said. "And I better go change." For the first time she felt that she had finally made a friend before Sasi could. That was made a big difference to her.

As Jamie was changing, Sasi walked up to her from behind. "Big deal you made a friend," she said. "Look, you should have learned how to swim all those times."

Jamie looked back.

"Sorry," Sasi said and walked away. Jamie thought the only person that knew she couldn't swim was Sasi. She looked to where Sasi was standing and quickly walked away to join Anna. Everyone liked Anna, mostly because she always was so bold. What they didn't like was that she won competitions against the fastest swimmers in school after they had boasted that they were going to win. Jamie just stood in the shallow end of the pool looking for Sasi just in case she was planning something. Then something dragged her into the water. Jane was the first to shout Jamie's name. Then everything went blurry and Jamie closed her eyes, as everything went black.

* * *

"Mom," Jamie said. She was at home. How did it happen? she wondered. "Aunt Midge's car is at school," Jamie said.

"I know," said her mom. "I have taken care of that. Rest," she said.

Jamie closed her eyes.

CHAPTER SIX

Cheaters

Jamie stayed at home for three days. She couldn't believe that Sasi had tried to drown her. She tried to help around the house but her mother thought she was too weak for that and didn't allow her to do much. Jamie sat on a chair as she took her hair band and dragged one of her ponytails into it. Her hair usually grew fast and the bands soon became loose. She did the same thing to the second ponytail and then combed them. There was a knock on the door.

"Come in," Jamie said. Her mother came in carrying cupcakes with banana icing: Jamie's favourite.

"Thanks," Jamie said as she grabbed one.

"Sasi is no more in that swimming place," her mom told her. "But I will make sure that you learn how to swim."

"Thanks, mom," Jamie said.

"You will be in school tomorrow. Do you think you can manage?"

"Yes, mom," Jamie said. "I will be fine. Can I go for a walk?"

"Of course," her mom said. "But whenever feel tired, come back home immediately."

"Okay, mom," said Jamie. She got her leather jacket and went outside. She opened the door and took another cupcake and then waved at her mother. She walked along the streets. It had been a long time since she got to walk outside for no reason. She walked past the bakery shop and then got to her school where she paused. How far have I walked? she thought and looked back. She was at her house. Jamie shook her head. She kept trying to think and then she rang the doorbell. Maybe I shouldn't go to school tomorrow, she thought.

"Jamie! Hey Jamie! I thought you were going for a walk," her mom said as she opened the door.

"I was at school," Jamie said, rubbing her head. "I think I will just go inside. I think my mind is getting foggy. I need to go back to bed."

"I left the cupcakes in your room," her mom said. But Jamie didn't hear her. She got to her bed and locked the door, opened a box and removed a silver button. She remembered the time she and Sasi her were best friends and did everything together. She accidentally removed the button out of her silver jacket, threw it to the floor and sighed. Could things ever go back to the way they used to be? she wondered.

At School

"Jamie," Anna said, "I came to your club. So did Preston. I thought Jane will go to Sasi but she did not. She is allergic to milk and Sasi came near her with chocolate. She kept on sneezing, even on Sasi's clothes. You should have been there. She called Jane a disease and Preston was there. I expected him to be furious but he just told Sasi that Jane was allergic to chocolate and the principal gave Sasi a long stare and you should see the hall where they are holding the party. We did it exactly the way you planned but a guy named Finn joined Sasi's club. I had to give him a little treatment."

"Slow down, Anna!' Jamie said. "It's nice to be back in school. Just tell me more later," Jamie said. "I can't believe gotta stay at home from school."

"Was it fun watching movies all day?" Anna said with a sparkle in her eyes.

"I kind of missed school," Jamie said. "It's fun and, after lunch, you can show me the place where you sorted out the competition."

"Sure," Anna said with a sign. "And everyone got crazy when they saw your aunt. You said she was a popstar but you never said she sang wicked. I can't sleep if I don't hear it all day. She is so good that even the principal asked for an autograph. I love that song oh!"

"Anna, let's go to class," Jamie said as she hurried up so that she would not be late.

At the Cafeteria

"Oh Anna! You want to sit with me and Jamie," Jane said. "I really like your design of the hall. I think you are going to win the competition and make Sasi suffer for ever calling me a disease," Jane said and swung her blackish blue and drank the milk on her tray out of a straw.

Jamie giggled. "Tell me about it. Every time a new kid sees Sasi they would go all best friends on her. Jane already saw the behavior of Sasi. She found a way to crack her to show her real identity."

Jamie giggled again. It was fun to know that Sasi's plan hadn't worked. She was probably thinking that if she got Anna, Jane and Preston my club will close shop, Jamie thought. She looked at Sasi. She was trying to get somebody's attention because she was dangling her earrings and blinking at someone but Jamie didn't care. "What flower are you planting?" she asked her.

Just then Sasi was at Jamie's table. She stopped and listened. Jamie was always good at planting; so, she had to have a flower that could win the competition for sure.

"I think I will go with a red drift rose, the one that is really red," Sasi said to herself. She got out her phone and messaged her dad: "DAD, CAN YOU TELL OUR GARDENER TO BUY A RED DRIFT WHATEVER ROSE IT IS FOR A SCHOOL PROJECT? AND MAKE IT REALLY RED. CALL ME WHEN YOU GET THIS." She turned back to Jamie's table. "Girl, I need a favour," she said.

After Lunch

"I like Jane," Jamie said.

"I like her too," Anna said as she poured her leftovers into a trashcan. Jamie was about to pour her milk into the trashcan when Sasi's friends said, "So, which flower are you planting?"

"I will say a red drift rose," Sasi answered. "They are really beautiful. I told my dad to buy the plant. No way am I going to get my nails dirty. She laughed and left.

Jamie squashed the milk carton in her hand. "I must beat Sasi in that flower contest because she copied me. I am going to tell the judges what she did," she said as she poured the leftover into the trashcan and left, with Anna trying to calm her down.

CHAPTER SEVEN

Inspiration

Jamie walked home together with Anna trying to think.

"Sasi just wants to win the competition. She could just plant the flower, make it grow and not try to cheat me," Jamie said.

"If she wants to cheat, just beat her at her game. You can cheat too!" Anna said.

"I am not going to be irresponsible or anything like that, although pushing Sasi into a pool would be really fun," Jamie said. "Anyway, she can't just cheat. And you heard her: she already got that rose." She saw a stone on the floor and stepped on it really hard, as if trying to crush it and let out her anger on it.

"It's okay, Jamie," Anna said. "How pretty can that rose be?"

"Oh! It's pretty all right. Here, let me show you a picture of it on my phone," Jamie said as she showed Anna a picture.

"Wow! Sasi is definitely going to win with that rose!" Anna said.

"Yes. It's sold right off the shelf without us even telling everyone about it. Whenever they go to the farm, cottonfield and flower shops, I'm going to tell the principal tomorrow," Jamie said and turned towards her house. "Bye, Anna. See you later," she said and entered her house. She lay down on a sofa reading a book about flowers, while trying to decide which flower to use.

The Next Day

Jamie walked to the principal's office.

"Jamie, what a wonderful surprise!" the principal exclaimed and took her glasses off her nose. "It's Sasi, isn't it?" she asked.

Jamie nodded.

"What did she do this time?" the principal asked.

"She copied my idea of what rose I wanted to plant, and bought it," Jamie said.

"I am so sorry, Jamie" the principal said. "I will give you two extra marks in whatever you do. I'll give you extra marks. I don't want to make her father angry. You know what he can do."

Then Sasi entered the principal's office. "Hello," she said. Her eyes fell on Jamie. "I wanted to say I found a flower. I told dad to order it already," she said.

Jamie twitched her eyes. She knew Sasi just wanted to annoy her.

"Oh Jamie! And I was just talking about that," Sasi said.

Jamie nodded with a smile that was forced. "I am sure whatever you are planting is wonderful," said Jamie with an even wider smile. She felt that if Sasi saw that she was happy despite the teasing, she will be annoyed.

"Anyway," the principal said, "I thought that since your club already set up the place, I should make the show more interesting. All of your members will compete against each other. I just finished writing the names of each of your members. You are going to compete with each other."

"Oh! I am going to buy a flower for all the people in my club then," Sasi said as she looked at the paper the principal handed them.

"No," the principal said. "I will allow you to buy anything. But do not do it for your members. And I will call their parents to see to that."

Sasi grunted. "But I will lose to a group of nerdos," she grumbled.

"You are dismissed," the principal said. "And there is a meeting after school today. So, go to your classes. I don't want you to miss Mathematics. And Sasi? Please keep your grades up," the principal concluded as she gently shoved them out of her office.

"Wow!" the principal said aloud to herself. "Children are a handful." And she went back to her seat and used a napkin to wipe her face.

* * *

Jamie got to her club late.

"I am sorry, everyone. Is anyone missing?" she asked.

"My brother," Jane said. "But he will come later. He was asking the Math teacher how to solve a problem. He always does that." Jane rolled her eyes.

"Sorry, I am late. I heard they already know. Jane!" shouted Jamie as she pointed to an empty seat next to Jane. "Preston went there anyway. The principal decided to make the show more interesting. So, you guys are competing with the other team. I just have two minutes to say who you are competing with. Please listen to the pairings. Anna and Angela, Preston and Mike, Jane and Chris, Miles and Finn, Dave and Sophie, Cassie and Grace, Emma and Sunshine, James and Drake, and Lilac and Lily.

"I want you to plant a flower each; and, on the day of the competition, bring it; and all of you should do your best."

Then the school bell rang.

"Bye, everyone," Jamie said as everybody, including her, rushed out of the school. Jamie saw her dad as she got out of the school.

"Anna, your parents said I should pick you up. And, congratulations! Your mom is pregnant," Jamie's dad said.

"What!" Anna exclaimed.

Jamie smiled at her and she smiled back. Jamie's dad took Anna to the hospital where her parents were, even though she didn't want to go.

Jamie and her dad then went home.

After dinner, Jamie locked herself up in her room and looked at her book of flowers and wished that her inspiration will come to her again. She fell asleep after doing her homework. She later woke up to a beautiful song of a bird with rainbow colours. She wasn't surprised. Normally, birds came every day because of the cottonfield and greenhouse nearby. It was so beautiful to hear the bird sing, and Jamie patted him on the head. It twisted away from her and flew away. Jamie thought of all the colorful flowers. A rainbow of flowers, no roses, she thought and called Anna to tell her about her idea. She also told her father who provided the seeds. She learned the Lincoln rose was the reddest rose there was.

Finally, there was a way to beat Sasi, thought Jamie.

CHAPTER EIGHT

Long Time No See

"Hi Jamie. How is the rainbow coming along?" Anna asked on the phone. Jamie had decided to call her. It had been two weeks and the Lincoln flower had decided not to bloom. "Sorry I can't hear you," she said to Jamie. "Jake!" Anna shouted. "Turn that thing off. I am trying to talk to someone."

Jamie heard a loud kindergarten song playing in the background. "Sorry, Jamie," Anna said. "It's Jake's birthday and we're stuck watching horrible baby rhymes. My older sister is in the mall buying shoes and clothes," Anna added, mimicking her sister's voice. "You can come to my house if you like, Jamie," said Anna.

"Hi Jamie," Anna's dad said.

Jamie was taken by surprise. "Hello," she said. "Is Anna still there?"

"No, she went outside," Anna's dad answered. "She said she is coming to your house. I think she is tired of having Jake beat her because of a cake."

"Sir, please say happy birthday to Jake for me," Jamie said and cut the call. She went outside and got a watering can. She filled it with water and then watered her golden yellow roses and orange roses, then her green roses and blue roses. She noticed that some blue roses were dying. She also watered her white roses. She thought of indigo and violet roses but knew she would need a very big pot and it will be too heavy.

Anna arrived Jamie's place with her own flowers. They were orange, yellow and golden flowers all mixed together.

"I hope all other members planted flowers and that they are growing really well," Jamie said. "I am so not sure my Lincoln red rose is ever going to bloom. I water it and give it attention every day but it is just not blooming."

"Maybe this is not right," Anna said. "I mean, it has too much water. It is so damp, Jamie. Your other flowers bloomed. This will bloom too. It will just take longer. Plus, with your Lincoln rose and your rainbow sparkle idea, they will definitely overshadow whatever flowers Sasi may bring. I am sure they are not doing as well as yours."

"I hope so," Jamie said. "Sasi has been here. I think she wants to see my flowers for herself. But I put a sign on some sunflowers saying they are for me. The next time I saw them, they had been stepped on with high heel boots."

"Smart thinking," Anna said. "But I still can't believe there are no blue roses. "Why didn't you water them? The contest is in two weeks."

"I already told you, Anna," said Jamie. "A blue flower is just a dying white flower. So, if I pour less water on it, it will become bluer. I won't let it completely die."

"I think your flower is so beautiful," Anna said. "It is definitely going to beat Sandra's. I hear Preston's father is very rich and he is best friends with a mayor."

Anna has been talking about Preston for a week, Jamie thought. She wanted a red car too. "Anna, I don't have a car. But you can take a driving test," Jamie said.

"No oh! forget it," Anna said.

"I wish I had a job like my sister. Then I won't have to babysit my brother," Jamie said. "Then I could go wherever I want."

"Oh, I understand," said Anna. "You want to be an only child. I am not sure it will be fun. Meanwhile, Preston's father, the mayor and the principal are coming. They are the judges of the contest.

"Oh shit!" Jamie said. "Sasi will probably tell her father to bribe him. What am I going to do?"

"How do you know that?" Anna asked.

"Sasi said it on the school teaching blog," Jamie replied.

"You follow the school?" asked Anna.

"Nope," Jamie said. "I use it to sleep when I am bored."

"Okay," Anna said. "So, you follow it."

"If you say so." Well, a lot of people in my club say that Sasi looked at my flowers. She really wants to impress the judges. She hopes her idea of a rainbow and white flower that looks like clouds will win the day, Jamie said to herself. But nobody is going to make me lose, not even Sasi. Then she looked at Anna and smiled.

"She is not going to make me lose," Jamie said. "I just know I am going to get back at her for cheating. I don't expect her to think much about that rose. I know Sasi. By the time she brings it to the competition it will be a little dry. Let's go inside. There is a pizza in the oven I made."

"Too bad you didn't get to make dinner for Aunty Midge," Anna said.

"I never wanted to," Jamie said. "Let's say it's a win for Sasi and me." She smiled and grabbed Anna's hand. "Come on! You came here for fun. Your flower is safe there. I will put it in the greenhouse."

But Anna had already gone inside. Jamie looked at the place she planted her flowers. Maybe I should put the flowers in the pot now, she thought. She looked at her Lincoln rose that had not yet bloomed. Please bloom, she prayed silently. Maybe I should leave the flower on the ground until the Lincoln flower grows. She took one last look at the flowers and carried Anna's flowers to the greenhouse. Then she joined Anna to eat the pizza and watch a movie.

"Why do you want a job?" Jamie asked Anna. "You said you wish you had a job, to get away from the house when mom tells Jack he can do whatever he wants whenever he is crying."

"It's his natural charm," Anna said. "My sister always says bye; I am late for work. I rushed out of the house and I am the one who has to do baby back rides all over the house. I am not sure my parents mind at all my being Jake's horse."

"But I do," Anna said. "He's trying to break my back."

When they got to her house, it was 6:30 pm. Jamie opened the door for Anna. Jake was asleep on the couch and Anna's parents were on the opposite side of the couch sleeping too. Anna entered her house tiptoeing and Jamie shut the door. Then she heard Jake say, "Anna is back."

Jamie laughed inside. Oh Anna! she thought. Thank God I am an only child.

CHAPTER NINE

Bloom

Jamie looked outside her windows and smiled. A smell was on the air like sweet flowers in bloom. It smelled like that yesterday, and her Lincoln rose still hadn't bloomed. She stood up from her bed and used a towel to wipe her face and then went to dress up.

Immediately she was done, she went outside. There was a little bud on the flower but no bloom. She knelt down beside the flowers and spoke tenderly.

"Why are you taking so long?" she asked. "I know you are still growing but the others have bloomed already. Can't you just grow? It is almost the day of the competition. I need to show Sasi that cheats never prosper. I hope I win just to show Sasi that cheating is bad. She might bribe the judges and I might even get the lowest score."

Talking to a rose is awkward, Jamie thought as she stood up. I will make breakfast, she decided as she walked back to her house. Sometimes her parents woke up late. Last time, when Anna was around, her dad was at the farm and her mom had gone to one of her businesses giving business advice and being the CEO of many companies. Her mom always worked later than her dad did. Most times, Jamie got back through the back door of the kitchen but her mother was there already checking her meatball and sauce filled with onions on the stove and spaghetti on another stove.

"I didn't know you woke up already. I woke up your father to dust the closet. I forgot to do it yesterday. I went to cook," Jamie's mother said with a yawn.

"You were fast," Jamie said.

"Oh! I am just warming up the one I cooked yesterday night while you were sleeping," said her mom.

"Okay," Jamie said. "You seem tired. You should have slept more."

"I know," her mom said. "Just eat the food on the table and let dad take you to school."

Jamie tried to eat but kept on thinking. Then she dropped her spoon. What if my plants never grow, she wondered. Oh! Face it! Jamie said to herself. Maybe I just lack faith. Then she saw her mom talking on the phone. I need to take a break from school so I can spend more time with my roses. And I will know why my Lincoln rose can't bloom or if I can just go outside and see my roses bloom just like that. But I won't get a visit from a rose fairy if there is such a thing. She groaned. She managed to finish her food.

School projects should be the least of your problems, she told herself. In high school enemies are many. Her dad was going to drive her to school. She checked on her rose again and poured a little water on it just in case it might help. Then her dad drove her to school.

On the way, he began to ask, "What about your ro – "

"Do not say that word, dad!" Jamie interrupted. "Yes, it's not going well. It's been two weeks and all I see is a bud and no bloom. How am I expected to win the contest? Then Sasi would not know that she just can't do anything like a wild girl who has no care in the world."

"Is it that bad?" Jamie's dad asked. "Maybe we should talk to your principal about this. She can do something about it. Think about it, okay."

"I get it," she said. But all Jamie thought about was winning. "I just have to win," she murmured and then groaned. When she got to school, she went to her locker and put some story books in it and then locked it. She remembered when she and Sasi used to share lockers. Now, Sasi had a golden locker and a silver one.

She always wanted one that was perfect for her but she said she was so beautiful she was the most perfect ever, Jamie thought.

Then she heard Sasi say something like, "I am going to win. I just know it."

"But what if you don't?" Claire her bff said.

"Then you can stop being my best friend," Sasi said. "I don't like losers anyway."

Sasi shook her head, swinging her long hair in Claire's face. Then she went past Jamie like she was not there.

"Hi!" Claire said to Jamie.

Jamie knew her to be friendly. She smiled at her.

For the first time in a long time, Jamie got through classes that day without thinking about her flowers. When it was closing time, she started to give up. When she got home, she watered the red rose. "I am pretty sure you won't grow anyways," she murmured. Then she washed her hands.

"So, what about your rose?" Jamie's mom asked her.

"It is dead," Jamie answered. "I am starting to think I am not really good at gardening."

Her mom and dad just looked at each other. "Losing doesn't mean anything," her dad said. It does not mean you cannot be great."

Jamie went to her room and lay on her bed. She was sad. "Too bad I can't win. I just wanted to show Sasi she can't win by cheating. But I guess mom's right: I can't win at everything." She slept off after sometime.

Jamie woke up a few minutes before 6 a.m. She had her bath, dressed up and went downstairs.

"Hi mom! Hi dad," she greeted her parents who were already up.

"Good morning, Jamie," said her dad. "Are you still sad about your flowers?"

"No, dad, but it hurts," Jamie said. "I will just go with yellow and orange, green and blue."

"Jamie, I think you should check the garden to water them," her mom said.

"Sure. Okay, I guess," Jamie said and went outside to check on her plants. When she saw her roses, she dropped the watering can in surprise.

CHAPTER TEN

Winners Got To Win And Losers Got To Lose

Jamie couldn't believe what she was looking at.

"I have finally grown a Lincoln flower! I can't believe it!" she squealed and jumped up for joy. "Now I can win the competition. I know I can. In two days' time I will win." She was so excited that even the air smelled sweeter to her than before.

It was still dawn. So, Jamie had time to water the plants. "I can't wait to get them into pots. I'm never going on YouTube ever again angry at Sasi," Jamie said to herself.

"Hello mom," Jamie said to her mother and kissed her on the cheek.

"Jamie, you greeted me before," her mom said.

"Sorry, mom. I thought I didn't," Jamie said. "And thanks for telling me to check the garden for no reason."

At School

"Hey Jamie! Where did you get those shoes from? A dumpster?" Sasi said when she saw Jamie.

"Oh no! In a shoe shop where I saw you buy those fancy shoes!" Jamie said.

Sasi turned red when she saw that Preston had heard her and walked past her. Jamie high-fived him as they stood to the opposite of each other. It seemed Jamie was starting to like Preston. He liked books and was not like those boys who cared only about riches and all of those stuffs.

"Who did your hair? A chimpanzee in art class?" Preston asked.

"Nope," Jamie said. She painted a picture of a peacock with a rainbow as its feather. "Sasi paid someone to do her painting. Oh! I am so going to win the competition."

"I can't believe it, okay," Preston said.

"I was joking at the moment," Jamie said.

"I know I am going to win anyway," Sasi said.

"Oh! I hope you have a cupboard to put it and I also hope your rash doesn't break out since you are allergic to sawdust," Jamie said. Sasi turned angry red.

"Why do you keep torturing me? Can't we both live in peace?" Jamie asked her. But Sasi just walked away. Jamie rolled her eyes. The only way you can annoy me is ruin my flowers, she thought as she also walked away. There was no club meeting that day. She did check if every flower had been planted correctly and watered. Sasi had her own club meeting that day. And she planned to give everyone a golden uniform. She said they had to look good to win.

Even the nicest clothes won't help you win in any gardening competition, Jamie thought. She didn't care about Sasi and her mean tricks.

Jamie's dad came to pick her up. Anna didn't come to school today, Jamie noted. I will check on her later when I'm done planting. "Hi dad," she said as she opened the car door quickly.

"I really want to go home, okay," Jamie's dad said. "You don't have to exaggerate. What's so special?"

"Oh, nothing. I just want to go home," Jamie said.

"Okay," her dad said and started the car. They soon got home. Immediately, Jamie ran to her garden to see her flowers. She ran to get a pot inside the house, then she dropped her bag in her room and fetched the pot. She took her rainbow roses in a round shape and white flower that looked like clouds.

"I know I can win," Jamie said aloud to herself. She carried her flower inside her room and put it by her window. At least, it is safe here, she thought.

"Jamie!" her mother called her. "It's time for dinner."

"Okay, mom," Jamie said. She went downstairs, went straight to the dining table and was about to open her plate.

"Jamie, go wash your hands," her mom said. "It is not appropriate to eat with dirty hands."

"Okay, mom," Jamie said as she entered the kitchen to wash her hands. She couldn't stop thinking about her flowers. It was so hard for her to wait for the next day. She couldn't even sleep as she tossed on the bed. Then she managed to fall asleep sometime later, dreaming of the colorful world of flowers.

* * *

The next day, there was a lot of cleaning of the place to be used for the contest. The chairs were decorated with flowers.

The place smelled like a garden of flowers. Jamie had a feeling that they had cleaned the place up at closing time the previous day. But it was worth all the hard work. The principal thanked the two clubs after they made the place sparkle. Jamie had gotten a good night's sleep even though she was nervous. She thought of Sasi bribing the judges and was very worried. But she was later able to calm down.

Thinking about beating Sasi made her comfortable, and she slept off after reading some books.

* * *

Finally, it was D-Day, the day the competition would hold.

Jamie woke up early. She decided to wear a white dress with flowers of different colors and types. For footwear, she chose flat shoes and a light blue jeans jacket. She looked at herself in the mirror and liked what she saw. Now, her hair. It had grown long. She thought of the time when her hair grew too long. It was so long that when she sat down, it touched the floor and people started calling her mop-floors. She had to pack her hair just so people won't call her that again.

Then she thought: I don't care about her anymore. She removed her hair bands and then combed her hair. Much better, she said to herself as her hair fell to her shoulders.

"Hey dad, hi mom," she called out to her parents after breakfast.

"Hey Jamie," her mom and dad said together. "You look fancy. Where are you going to?" her dad asked when he saw she was in a rush.

"You know, dad. Can you take me to school now?" Jamie asked him after she finished her breakfast.

"Okay," her dad said.

Jamie got her bag and her plant. She did not want Sasi to see it, so she put it in a nylon bag.

When she got to school, Jamie went to the greenhouse and dropped her plant. Luckily, she was early and nobody was there. She smiled. I can't wait for the competition, she thought.

"Hi Jamie," Preston said.

"Oh! I thought you were someone else," Jamie said.

"Wow! Your hair is really long," he said.

"Thanks," she said. "Can I see your flowers?" Jamie asked.

"Sure," he said and showed her a red flower shaped like a heart.

"Wow! That is beautiful," Jamie said.

"Yeah, my father is a tough judge. So, I want to really impress him. He's not really at home so much. So, I have to take Jane every place I go," Preston said.

Jamie laughed.

"Where are your flowers?" Preston asked as he dropped his flowers where there was not too much sunshine.

"Oh! I was saving them because Sasi crushed my other flowers. I guess I can trust you," Jamie said. "Here." She showed Preston and then put it back quickly where it was sunny and cool.

"Wow!" Preston said.

Then Jamie heard the honking of a car. "Sasi is here," she said. She and Preston walked out of the greenhouse

"What is up with you and Sasi? Can't you be friends?" Preston asked her.

"We used to be best friends. Suddenly, when her dad became a mayor, she dumped me just because I am not extremely rich like her," Jamie said.

They noticed that the number of students that were outside the school had grown. Mostly, they were members of Sasi's team. They were all dressed in gold-coloured clothes.

"Wow, Sasi!" Jamie said. "You sure know how to plan your things."

"Oh no, Jamie!" Sasi replied. "My real dress is in my bag, mop floor." She walked past Jamie and Preston with a covered tray. Sasi looked Jamie in the eye. "And, yes, that is my winning flower at the back of me," she said.

"I can't believe you two were actually friends," Preston said.

"Do you think I believe it myself?" Jamie said.

Later in class Sasi was asked to put her flower in the greenhouse. But she said that it needed a special spot. So, it was taken outside and put where only Sasi could go; and, everywhere she went, her teammates followed her saying she was going to win.

"I thought it was teamwork. Sasi isn't the one going to represent everyone," Jamie murmured.

It was night when the competition started. Parents came to celebrate spring. The school opened the roof for fresh air to come in. Jamie looked around;

Anna wasn't there. She was worried. She had forgotten to check on her yesterday. Now there was crying behind her from a boy. Jamie tuned around. Anna was there with her flower and her mom and Jake.

"Anna!" Jamie whispered as loudly as she could manage. The MC was speaking and introducing the judges, and she did not want to call attention to herself.

"Hi Jamie. I am sorry I didn't call. There was poor network in the hospital," Anna said.

Jamie saw her mom was still pregnant. "Where's your elder sister?" she asked.

"She has been sneezing so much. She had a headache. She is not okay," Anna said.

"Maybe she is allergic to flowers," Jamie said. "Anyway, we are here," she told Anna, showing her their position.

"Where is Sasi?" Anna asked.

"She wants to make a grand entrance," Jamie said. She took her flower from Jane. "Thanks for holding it for me," she said.

"You are welcome," Jane answered.

"Let me introduce the contestants," the MC said. "Let the competition begin! Please welcome Jane and Chris!

Jane went up the platform. The judges inspected her flowers. Jane got low scores. But her father did give her a five.

"You did well," Jamie said.

"I know," Jane said, smiling.

How come she is never sad? Jamie thought. After two more contestants were judged, it got to Jamie and Sasi's turns. The whole time, Jamie's club had won, won and won.

Sasi walked up in a cloud of smoke wearing a red dress. Then Jamie came up next. They were asked to show the crowd their flowers and then the judges.

"I give this a six," the mayor said. "Don't you agree?" he said to his friend. He is trying to convince him to support his choice, Jamie thought. But, of course, he can't bribe a famous person; that will make him look bad.

"I give it a nine. Great work with the rainbow," he said. The principal smiled.

"I give it a ten."

Oh! Top score! thought Jamie. Will Sasi be able to beat her?

Sasi showed her flower to the mayor first. He gave her an eight. Sasi looked angry. But Jamie was not surprised. She knew that if he had given her a ten, his friend would think he did not bring up his child with discipline, and that was true.

"Hmm. It's a little wilted. I will give you a four." The principal gave Sasi a six. After that they up added each club's total scores.

"I want to announce the winner," the MC said. 'And the winner is . . . Jamie!"

Jamie And the Flower Contest

Jamie went up to collect her golden trophy. "I win!" she shouted. Then her club members carried her up shouting, "Winner! Winner! Winner!"

Meanwhile, Sasi was angry. "Let's go home, daddy," she said and left even before her dad could stand up. Jamie's parents came up and kissed her on her cheeks.

After the competition Jamie's family went out to celebrate the trophy. They got home very tired. Jamie went to her room while her parents watched the news. She called Anna on the phone. "I won!" she said.

"I guess it means winners get to win and losers get to lose, and you're the winner. Congrats, Jamie. And bye. I have to help Jake; he can't open the cupboard. But why did the school give me a blue ribbon saying Number One when you got the trophy?"

Oh! Anna!" Jamie laughed and cut the call. She looked at the golden trophy on her desk with fake flowers, turned off the light and fell asleep.

Today was the first day of spring.

The End

ABOUT THE BOOK

When the principal of a modest suburban primary school announced to her students a flower-planting contest to be held among them and to be judged by an elite panel of judges, she was certain of producing future horticulturists and agriculturists as well as competitive and excellence-driven individuals in general. But there was another certainty: she did not factor in the drama that such a contest will create among the young contestants who collided in a heady mix of love, friendship and cooperation, envy, jealousy and hate; drama so intense that, at times, it verged on the very deadly.

ABOUT THE AUTHOR

Grace Inioluwa Shobola was born on August 1, 2013 as the firstborn of her parents. Outside her curricular activities, Grace enjoys reading and writing short stories. She is presently in Grade 6 at County Crest School, Mowe in Ogun State, Nigeria. She loves flowers a lot, a love that inspired this book which is her first to be published.

www.ingramcontent.com/pod-product-compliance
Lightning Source LLC
Chambersburg PA
CBHW030621070426
42449CB00041B/987